Original title:
Rustle of Rhymes

Copyright © 2025 Creative Arts Management OÜ
All rights reserved.

Author: Eleanor Prescott
ISBN HARDBACK: 978-1-80567-431-3
ISBN PAPERBACK: 978-1-80567-730-7

Breezes that Sing Forgotten Tales

In the park, a squirrel pranced,
Chasing shadows, never chanced.
A breeze whispered a joke quite bold,
As leaves rolled laughter, bright and gold.

A cat named Mittens took a leap,
Fell in a puddle, made a deep beep.
The ducks all quacked, and oh, what fun!
An audience formed, smiles all spun.

Harmonies Entwined with Nature's Breath

Buzzing bees in a silly row,
Dancing high and moving slow.
A sunflower grinned, sun's best friend,
Winking at bees 'round the bend.

A frog on a lily, singing high,
Croaked out a tune, who knew why?
Butterflies twirled, just for a glance,
In this wacky, whimsical dance.

Threads of Time in Poetic Motion

Tick-tock, the clock plays a prank,
Hours skitter like a potato tank.
The old man chuckles, strikes a pose,
His glasses slip, where nobody knows.

With every moment, puns abound,
A clockwork jelly rolls 'round and 'round.
Time winks mischievously at me,
While giggling squirrels race to be free.

Rhapsody of Leaves and Laughter

Autumn leaves dance in a twist,
Each spin a soggy, leafy mist.
A child throws them, dances around,
As laughter paints the autumn ground.

In the air, a funny tune,
Sung by a raccoon, under the moon.
He slips on acorns, makes a fuss,
A comedy show—who needs a bus?

Syllables in the Breeze

Words waltz on the air, quite silly and spry,
They tickle the trees as they giggle and fly.
A pun in the branches, a rhyme in the breeze,
Each chuckle and snicker brings joy with such ease.

Chirping with laughter, the sparrows join in,
Syllables dancing with a whimsical grin.
The whispers of verses take flight, oh so bright,
While clouds poke their heads, trying not to ignite.

Fluttering Stanzas

Stanzas take flight like a kite in full sway,
They twirl in the sunlight, come out to play.
One lands on a fence, another on a hat,
With giggles and wiggles, they chat just like that.

Silly metaphors bounce on the grass,
Each line is a joke, hoping none will surpass.
A chorus of laughter erupts from a bee,
As it sips from a flower, so carefree and free.

Lullaby of Laughter

Close your eyes, hear the chuckles so sweet,
As rhymes tiptoe softly on tiny bare feet.
A lullaby sung by the moon in delight,
While stars wink at jokes that twinkle at night.

Tickles and giggles weave into dreams,
Where marshmallows dance in candy-coated beams.
The owls hoot in rhythm, a funny refrain,
As they join in the chorus of joy and of rain.

Breezy Ballad

A ballad in breezes that tickle the trees,
Brings laughter to blossoms and buzz to the bees.
With a skip and a hop, the verses take flight,
While chiming with glee, they dance through the night.

Each rhyme is a feather, so light and so free,
They drift on the air, just as happy can be.
With smiles all around, in a comical spree,
This breezy ballad sings joy endlessly.

Embrace of the Evening

When the sun gives a wink, and the moon starts to prance,
Squirrels adjust their ties, ready for the dance.
A cat in a bow tie takes the center stage,
With mice as the band, they all engage.

Stars twinkle like lights on a disco ball,
While fireflies hum, having a ball.
The crickets all chirp in a humorous tune,
And a raccoon juggles while hooting at the moon.

Joyful colors of dusk paint the sky just right,
As friends tell their jokes, filling up the night.
With laughter like music drifting through the trees,
The evening unfolds with an easy breeze.

So let's raise a toast to the quirky delight,
To chaos and laughter that spark up the night.
In the embrace of the evening, let worries all fade,
For a world full of giggles is joyfully made.

Glimmers of the Gloaming

As the sunset ignites colors all around,
The frogs start their croaking, a symphonic sound.
With crickets auditioning for a grand play,
The night air is thick with a silly ballet.

A raccoon with glasses reads poems aloud,
While owls take notes, tremendously proud.
The shadows do twist and take on a twist,
In this dance of the night, nobody's missed.

Star-shaped cookies are served on a tray,
With lemonade rivers that swirl and sway.
The whispers of mischief echo the still,
As fireflies party and twinkle at will.

So grab your odd hat and join in the fun,
In the glimmers of gloaming, the laughter won't run.
With squirrels in tuxedos and jokes being spun,
This is the magic when day is all done.

Spheres of Sentiment

In circles of joy where the laughter splits,
Balloons take a ride, and the giggles commit.
The cats wear monocles, sipping their tea,
A chorus of fables spring forth so carefree.

With puns in the air like confetti in flight,
Each corner holds secrets, shadows holding tight.
The friends gather 'round under a blanket of stars,
Playing charades while pretending to spar.

A puppy named Pickles runs into the scene,
Wearing a cape and a crown, like a dream.
With tumbling antics, he's the star of the show,
In spheres of sentiment where tomfoolery flows.

So let's relish this moment, let laughter unwind,
For joy is a treasure, rare and unconfined.
These spheres filled with giggles become our own bliss,
In the web of this night, let fun be our kiss.

Whims of Whispers

In the corner of twilight, whispers take flight,
As the shadows conspire with hilarious might.
The moon smirks and grins, as if in on the jest,
While the breeze carries secrets from east to the west.

A kangaroo hops by, juggling three pies,
With a look of confusion that's hard to despise.
The owls start to hoot, creating a sound,
Of laughter and mischief that's echoing 'round.

Giggles break loose from behind every tree,
As shadows play tag, oh, can you see?
With a twinkling grin, the night creatures sing,
In the whims of whispers, joy is the king.

So relish this breath of delight on the cusp,
As the giggles and whispers embrace like a gust.
In the gentle caress of the night's soft caress,
Find humor and laughter, we're truly blessed.

Verses Flowing Like a Mountain Stream

Words dance lightly like a breeze,
Silly tales bring us to our knees.
A fish in a hat? Oh what a sight!
Laughter bubbles in the soft twilight.

Bouncing ideas like stones on water,
A joke told by a friendly otter.
Tickling trees with their playful sway,
Funny whispers brighten up the day.

Mossy rocks giggle, can you hear?
Each verse flows, from ear to ear.
The moon winks, as if in on the jest,
We wander in whims, feeling so blessed.

Crossing streams in mismatched shoes,
Polka-dot frogs share their vivid views.
In this giggling brook, we float and beam,
Life's funny moments, like a happy dream.

Songs of Old Told in New Ways

Once upon a time in a shoe,
A giant sneezed and out sprang a crew.
Fairy tales told with a twist so bright,
Now involve dragons who dance at night.

A prince named Fred, who liked to bake,
Cakes and pies made the kingdom shake.
His whisk did twirl like a knight's sword,
Culinary quests with a humorous chord.

The princess chuckled at her plight,
Stuck in a tower, craving a bite.
She texted a dragon, "Bring me some chow!"
Their friendship bloomed, oh, what a wow!

In this realm, old ends meet new fate,
Funny tales travel, they always create.
With laughter and cake, they all sing along,
Echoing joy in their silly song.

Enchantment in the Rustling Canopy

In the woods where the squirrels play,
A tree spoke jokes in a leafy way.
With branches waving like they've got sass,
Every leaf giggled, like a sweet glass.

A fairy fluffed her sparkly hair,
Told all her pals, "Life's quite a fair!"
A mushroom and squirrel held a dance-off,
With their tiny steps, they made us scoff.

The sun tossed rays, like confetti in air,
While woodland creatures giggled everywhere.
A wise old owl wore glasses too small,
Preached wisdom, but forgot his call.

And as night fell, the stars took flight,
Twinkling with laughter, oh what a sight!
Under this canopy, we find delight,
In enchanted moments, both silly and bright.

Strophes Amidst the Summer's Caress

With summer breezes that tickle our toes,
We dance in the sun where the wildflower grows.
Ants in a parade, carrying crumbs galore,
Little explorers always wanting more.

Picnics of laughter spread out on the grass,
While bees in their bowties buzz through the mass.
Each sandwich tells stories, each fruit takes the stage,
As giggles and crumbs turn the book of our age.

Under the skies where the clouds poke fun,
We chase after rainbows, we sprint, and we run.
Lemonade laughter drips down from our cups,
Funny little moments, we savor in gulps.

At night we gather, the stars shining bright,
We share silly tales under the soft moonlight.
In summer's embrace, oh what fun it'll be,
The strophes of laughter, forever carefree.

Cadence of the Cosmos

In the cosmos, stars do waltz,
With comets that trip and somersaults.
Saturn wore rings made of cheese,
While aliens giggled with ease.

Planet Earth, it spun with flair,
Singing songs in the cosmic air.
A moonbeam slipped on a cosmic shoe,
Dancing under skies so blue.

Galaxies twirl in cosmic fife,
Creating chaos, full of life.
Each twinkle's a note in the night,
A symphony crafted in delight.

So let's spin with stars so bright,
Bouncing along in sheer delight.
Cosmic beats and silly sights,
In this rhythm of galactic flights.

Lament of Lost Lyrics

In a drawer, the lyrics hide,
Buried under socks, they bide.
Cats meow to an offbeat tune,
As a dog tries to hum a rune.

Papers crumpled, words out of place,
My mind ponders in a silly race.
I'd sing the blues with a rubber duck,
While rhymes just giggle and say, "What luck!"

Keyboards clatter with a sneeze,
As rhymes escape just like bees.
Sing a chorus of silly sounds,
While lost lyrics dance in bounds.

So I scribble and I laugh,
At words that vanished, what a gaffe!
With dreams of songs I may create,
While my lyrics just take a break.

Sonorous Secrets

In whispers soft, the secrets told,
Of moonlit dances and dreams of gold.
A squirrel played flute, a crow gave beats,
While turtles jived on tiny feets.

Mountains chuckled, clouds bounced around,
As laughter echoed without a sound.
Each pebble chimed a tune so fine,
Making mischief in rhythm divine.

Wind carried tales of the silly kind,
Of fish that walked, and birds that rhymed.
A serenade to those who dare,
To join in fun amidst the air.

So dance with me through skies so vast,
In a world where moments are cast.
Sonorous secrets fill the night,
With every chuckle, all feels right.

Voices Amongst the Vines

Gathered vines, they twist and twirl,
With giggles sprouting in a whirl.
Chubby grapes, they sway and swing,
As laughter blooms in the spring.

Every leaf has a whispering tale,
Of lazy bees and a drunk snail.
A sunflower grinned in the breeze,
As chirps of joy came with ease.

The garden hosted a concert grand,
With carrots dancing hand-in-hand.
Voices rose through leafy trails,
As nature's chorus filled the gales.

So come and dance 'neath trellised vines,
Join the fun where laughter shines.
In this haven where we play,
Voices mingle, come what may.

Melody Beneath the Boughs

Under the tree, a squirrel sings,
Bouncing along with shiny rings.
He dances and spins, quite the sight,
Nutty and quirky, brings sheer delight.

Leaves laugh softly to the tune,
As shadows waltz beneath the moon.
A playful breeze tickles the ground,
Where giggles and gaffes can always be found.

Shadows of Stanzas in the Wind

Words take flight, like silly birds,
Chasing each other, without any words.
Sentences tumble, a comic parade,
Riding the wind where laughter's made.

Puns float by in a whimsical whirl,
Tickling the trees, giving them a twirl.
Limericks linger, causing a grin,
As shadows of stanzas dance on a whim.

Verse in the Twilight Breeze

Twilight giggles, whispers in rhyme,
Tickling toes, in a jolly time.
Verse skips along on a merry spree,
Bringing back jokes from the old oak tree.

Silly shadows sneak in the light,
Dancing around, full of delight.
Chasing each other, they tumble and fall,
Making us chuckle, quite the ball!

Secrets Carried on Paper Wings

Paper planes soar with secrets untold,
Winged whispers of laughter, pure gold.
With each gentle flap, mischief takes flight,
While readers chuckle deep into night.

Jokes ride the currents, a whimsical chase,
Scribbled in margins, with playful grace.
A world of giggles, where puns take a spin,
On paper wings, let the fun begin!

Muses in Motion

In a world where ideas dance,
Silly thoughts take their chance.
Words wiggle and twirl about,
Chasing giggles, no doubt!

Puns play hopscotch on the page,
While rhymes dress up in even-age.
A hiccup of verse brings cheer,
Making laughter loudly clear!

Quills tickle, so they prance,
Searching for the perfect chance.
To leap and skip with much glee,
In a jolly jamboree!

Amidst the fun, they rhyme and tease,
Blowing bubbles in the breeze.
With each line, the jests engage,
Creating joy on every stage!

Streams of Serenity

In a stream where thoughts abound,
Silly fish flip, twist around.
Words float by like paper boats,
Making laughter—oh, it gloats!

Waves giggle at the shore,
Tickling toes forevermore.
The sun winks with a bright cheer,
As silly rhymes draw near!

Grassy banks wear hats of green,
Watching antics, oh so keen.
The sky chuckles, clouds applaud,
While froggy friends sing and nod!

Rippling laughter, oh what fun,
Under the lazy afternoon sun.
With each line a wave of joy,
Nature sings, oh what a ploy!

Sonnet of Shadows

In shadows where the giggles hide,
A playful jest does abide.
Whispers of silliness unfold,
In a tale that's often told.

Darkness wears a jolly grin,
While whispers dance, they twist and spin.
Ghosts in costumes of delight,
Spook the serious into fright!

With each shadow plays a joke,
The moonlight giggles, seldom choked.
As leaves giggle, dance or sway,
In a merriment display!

So come and join the shadowed fun,
Underneath the starlit run.
In rhymes that bounce and glide,
The humor serves as our guide!

Breeze-Kissed Metaphors

With breezes that tickle and tease,
Metaphors float like dancing leaves.
Words chase the wind in high glee,
As laughter echoes merrily.

Sailboats of phrases glide on air,
Spinning tales without a care.
Each pun a kite that flies on by,
Painting smiles across the sky!

Playful whispers twirl and spin,
Sending silly thoughts from within.
With each gulp of joyous breeze,
The tongue does loop in playful ease!

So let us skip on breezy lines,
And share the laughter in the pines.
For in these moments, light and free,
The rhythm's joy is the key!

Narrative Notes

In a world where socks play hide,
Gnomes steal snacks with goofy pride.
Toasters toast with burnt delight,
And cats dance in the moonlit night.

Frogs wear crowns and jump in pools,
Chasing dreams, while breaking rules.
Chickens gossip on the run,
Laughing loud, oh what a fun!

Whales sing songs on land, you see,
As elephants sip their herbal tea.
The sun wears shades, all cool and bold,
Telling stories that never get old.

So grab your pen, make notes galore,
Of dancing words, a silly score.
For every note, a giggle's found,
In the rhymes that spin around.

Palpitations of the Past

There once was a time, a fishing hare,
Caught dreams in nets without a care.
He'd wink at the moon with a cheeky grin,
While wearing a hat, that was too thin.

Old tigers wrote love letters loud,
To shadows dancing in a crowd.
Chasing memories on roller shoes,
In a world where the colors amuse.

Polka dots on a velvet sky,
Made all the cows dream they could fly.
They giggled and mooed, with such flair,
As balloons floated high, free as air.

So let's rewind and take a look,
At silly tales in our storybook.
With every heartbeat from those days,
Laughter echoes in funny ways.

Mirage of Metaphors

In a meadow where shoes can walk,
Pineapples gather for a talk.
They share their secrets, sweet and bright,
Under the stars, they sip moonlight.

A pink elephant juggles dreams,
While jellybeans float down in streams.
Cats wear ties at the tea-time,
Sipping laughter like it's prime.

The clouds form shapes of silly things,
Kites with wings and invisible springs.
Daisies whisper to the breeze,
In a language that's sure to tease.

So join this dance, this playful rhyme,
Where metaphors tumble through time.
With every twist and every twirl,
Life's a game in this funny swirl.

Woven Whispers

In a forest of yarn and strings,
Where squirrels plot and laughter rings.
A tapestry of giggles weaves,
Around the trees, where mischief leaves.

Toadstools tickle the feet of deer,
While rabbits burst with uncontained cheer.
The wind tells secrets, old and new,
Of whimsical tales, for me and you.

Jellyfish summon a marching band,
With clowns on stilts, oh isn't it grand?
The moonlight casts a funny glow,
On dancing shadows, putting on a show.

So stitch your dreams with threads of fun,
In a world where worries come undone.
For in these whispers, life's a jest,
A woven tale that's simply the best.

Whirlwinds of Thought in Dappled Light

In the garden of giggles, cats dance,
Chasing shadows, they spin, they prance.
Squirrels debate on who's the best,
While flowers laugh, they're on a quest.

Butterflies giggle, what a sight,
Bouncing on breezes, oh what a flight.
Sunbeams tickle, making things bright,
In this carnival of pure delight.

Bumblebees buzz, they sing their tune,
Whispering secrets like a funny cartoon.
Juggling raindrops, they make it sweet,
Dancing in circles, they can't be beat.

So come join the fray, don't delay,
In this wacky world, we laugh and play.
With thoughts like whirlwinds, take a bite,
In dappled light, everything feels right.

Choreography of Echoes and Dreams

A frog leaps high with a splashy sound,
While the snail moves slow, like it's spellbound.
Their dance is silly, oh what a show,
In the theater of grass, they steal the glow.

The moon winks down, playing coy,
As crickets chirp jigs, oh what joy!
Fireflies twinkle in rhythmic sway,
Guiding the night in a playful ballet.

Clouds turn into animals, oh dear,
Lions and ducks, become very clear.
The wind joins in with a whoosh and a twirl,
Creating a dream that makes you whirl.

So if you hear echoes of laughter and fun,
Join the choreography, don't you shun!
Let dreams take flight on this crazy beam,
In the moonlit night, life is a dream.

Syllables Sailing the Serene Sea

Words on waves, making a splash,
Floating along, they have a bash.
With giggles like ripples, they tease the shore,
Sailing in rhythm, they always want more.

Seagulls squawk jokes, with a wink of a wing,
As sailors recount every silly fling.
Billowing whispers and stories so grand,
In the tide of laughter, we make our stand.

Bubbles rise high, and so do the smiles,
Drifting together across ocean miles.
Each syllable dances, crafted just right,
In the serene sea, joy takes its flight.

So hoist up the sails, let laughter lead,
On waves of words, we're planted like seeds.
The sea sings sweetly, let it be known,
In the ocean of fun, we're never alone.

Notes Carved in the Bark of Trees

In the forest where songs take shape,
The trees tell tales of a funny drape.
Each groove and notch holds whispers tight,
Squirrels read them under the soft moonlight.

Woodpeckers drum like a band in the woods,
Raccoons chime in, oh how they could!
Bark becomes paper, the stories unfold,
With laughter and joy, so never grow old.

Autumn leaves rustle as they speak,
Of comical moments, oh so unique.
Each swirl and twirl, a funny phase,
In the library of nature, all get a gaze.

So listen closely, as the forest sings,
With notes in the bark, joy always clings.
In this treehouse of humor, we feel so free,
Nature's own symphony, come, hear with glee.

Song of the Seasons

Spring brings blooms in every hue,
A squirrel dons a tiny shoe.
Summer's heat makes ice cream melt,
While bees play songs that must be felt.

Autumn leaves, a crunchy sound,
Ghosts in costumes swirl around.
Winter's chill with snowflakes spry,
On penguins' dance, we laugh and sigh.

Twilight Terza Rima

The moon peeks out with a giggly glare,
A cat in shades lounges aware.
Stars wiggle bright like savory treats,

A chorus of crickets take the stage,
As frogs recite in a poet's rage.
Nighttime whispers in layers of beats.

The owls hoot jokes that drift on air,
With fireflies twinkling, they tease and dare.
A night of whimsy, a joyous page.

Glistening Glissandos

The piano keys dance a silly jig,
While frogs leap high, all smooth and big.
A tuba toots like a trumpet sneeze,
And cats weave rhythms in playful tease.

Maracas shake in a fanciful beat,
As laughter echoes down the street.
Conductor hats on our heads we wear,
As socks play tunes with a style to spare.

Jingling bells and clanging cans,
Making music with our pans.
Join the fun, as we leap and glide!

Nimbus of Narratives

In clouds above, stories unfold,
Of superheroes brave and bold.
A chicken flies to save the day,
With vegetable sidekicks in a fray.

Rain drops whisper quirky tales,
Of fish on bikes that ride the gales.
While umbrellas dance in the swirling wind,
Sketching plots where laughter's pinned.

Every story, a merry spin,
With giggles echoed from within.
A wondrous world where fun's the guide!

Streaming Sonorities

In a world where notes collide,
Melodies dance side by side.
Banjos strum and trumpets squeak,
Laughter's found in every peak.

Waltzes turn into wild swings,
When cats decide to play with strings.
Accordion sighs and flutes reply,
While fish begin to croon and fly.

Piano keys jump like they can fly,
With ducks in suits that do not try.
Every sound becomes a twist,
In this orchestra's playful mist.

The rhythm's silly, the tunes a game,
Every note is quite the same.
So join the fun, don't be a bore,
Let laughter ring forevermore.

Elegance of Echoes

In a hall where whispers prance,
Echoing tunes lead the dance.
Silly shadows sway and shake,
As giggles from the corners wake.

A trumpet toots, a bassoon honks,
While hippos sing in silly frocks.
Dapper moles in bow ties twirl,
Creating mischief with a whirl.

Banjos strum beneath the moon,
As frogs croak out a funny tune.
The elegance is quite absurd,
Like cats who think they're birds unheard.

Join the fun, it's all a jest,
In this echo, we are blessed.
Let your voice join the glorious row,
Of laughter making history glow.

Dappled Daydreams

In gardens bright where daisies dream,
Squirrels plot a silly scheme.
With acorns launched and fluffy tails,
Their antics weave incredible trails.

Butterflies in bowler hats,
Flutter by with witty chats.
They whisper tales of candy trees,
And dance with all the buzzing bees.

Sunshine glimmers on the brook,
As fish in tuxedos take a look.
They wiggle and giggle, making waves,
While frogs play chess in their green caves.

In daydreams bold where laughter blooms,
Every flower jests with plumes.
Join the dappled, bright parade,
In whimsy's magic that won't fade.

Chronicles of the Chiaroscuro

In shadows cast by vibrant light,
Giraffes in tuxedos take to flight.
With pastels danced on every wall,
They share silly tales, one and all.

As paintings twirl, a canvas sings,
With mustaches made from giant springs.
Art comes alive, with colors bold,
In stories of mischief, uproarious and old.

Ink spills over, creating delight,
While penguins dance, both day and night.
Brush strokes leap with a giggle and cheer,
In the chiaroscuro, joy's always near.

So come along and take a peek,
Where shadows chuckle and colors speak.
In this gallery of quirky fun,
The chronicles have only begun.

Scattered Sonnets Under the Stars

Stars giggle in the night sky,
Dancing like fireflies gone shy.
The moon winks with a cheeky grin,
While comets race, let the fun begin.

A sonnet slips from my pen,
Tripping over its rhymes again.
Words tumble like clumsy fools,
In the starry playground of verbal schools.

Each couplet hops, then takes a dive,
A whimsical yarn, where dreams thrive.
Laughter echoes through stardust air,
As verses float without a care.

Oh, to scribble under cosmic light,
With silly quips that take to flight.
In this arena, we rhyme and jest,
Each line a chuckle, each word a jest.

Musings of the Wandering Wind

The wind whispers secrets, just for fun,
Tickling the leaves, making them run.
It plays tag with the clouds above,
A breezy game, filled with love.

Chasing shadows, it twirls around,
Singing songs of silliness, profound.
Whirling through trees, it loves to tease,
Turning staid moments into a breeze.

"Catch me if you can," it laughs and shouts,
As it twines through all the curious doubts.
A playful gust, full of cheer,
Spreading giggles for all to hear.

In swirling whispers of air so light,
The wandering wind shares its delight.
With every gust, a ticklish rhyme,
Frolicking through the fabric of time.

Cadence of Clouds and Dreams

Clouds gather, fluffy and grand,
They paint shapes with a wispy hand.
A lion here, a pie over there,
A cotton candy world of air.

In dreamlike dances, they sway and spin,
Wrapping around the chortles within.
A circus up where giggles float,
On every cloud, a silly quote.

As I lounge and watch them drift,
My thoughts are carried, a whimsical gift.
Each puff a story, a laughter line,
In the soft spots where ideas entwine.

With every shift, a chuckle is born,
A carnival ride by morning's dawn.
In this dance of joy, I find my seams,
Weaving laughter into the fabric of dreams.

Sonorous Steps on the Path of Words

Walking on a path where the words play,
   Each step a giggle leading the way.
   With puns placed beneath my toes,
   Every tread is where humor grows.

   Each syllable hops and twirls about,
    In a rhythm that leaves no doubt.
   "Step right up!" the verses proclaim,
With cheerful voices calling my name.

I stumble on rhymes, fall into laughter,
   The road ahead is filled with banter.
     Every phrase a merry song,
     As I skip along all day long.

   Oh, the journey that words can take,
With a blunder or two for laughter's sake.
   In this sonorous dance of delight,
   I'll skip 'til I see the morning light.

Verse Under the Moon

The night is bright, the stars so spry,
A cat starts dancing, oh my, oh my!
The moon is laughing, a jolly sight,
While owls rehearse their jokes tonight.

A mice brigade whirls round the cheese,
With tiny hats, they giggle with ease.
A frog hops in with a grand old tale,
While crickets chime in, without fail.

The breeze is playful, the shadows leap,
While sleepy bats giggle and peep.
The fireflies twinkle, a flickering grin,
As they join the party, where fun begins!

So if you're lonely, just peek outside,
Join in the laughter, let joy be your guide.
For under the moon, good cheer flows bright,
With silly antics that spark pure delight.

Whirlwind of Whimsy

In a land where giggles grow on trees,
We sail on laughs carried by the breeze.
A squirrel in boots takes a leap and twirls,
While birds on bicycles race and twirl.

The flowers sway, wearing silly hats,
They dance with bees and play with bats.
A toad in a tutu hops along the lane,
Shouting 'Life is silly!' in a comical strain.

Bubbles of laughter float high in the sky,
As bubbles of bubbling stew start to fly.
A jester juggles jellybeans with flair,
While kids throw confetti in midair.

Catch a kite made of jokes and puns,
Let it soar high, oh what fun runs!
In this whirlwind of whimsy, we twirl and glide,
With laughter our ticket, let joy be our guide.

Swaying Spaces

In swaying spaces where breezes giggle,
A snail in a top hat starts to wiggle.
Chasing a shadow, it slips and falls,
Laughter erupts from the tiny walls.

Dancing daisies play peek-a-boo,
While ants wear boots and march in a queue.
The sun wears shades with a dazzling grin,
As clouds tickle it, let the fun begin!

A piñata tree bursts with candy galore,
While squirrels sneak under, their cheeks they store.
The bumblebees buzz in a jazzy tune,
As giggles echo through afternoon.

So sway with the rhythm, let laughter unfold,
In this silly place where joy is gold.
For in swaying spaces, friends gather 'round,
To share in the giggles, where fun can abound.

Alliteration in Autumn

Amidst amber leaves, a fox wears plaid,
With laughter that loops, it makes you glad.
Pumpkins are prancing, all dressed in cheer,
As squirrels crack jokes, their voices clear.

Whirling winds whisk through whimsical woods,
Dancing with deer in their cozy hoods.
Chasing the chill, they leap and bound,
With giggles and grins echoing around.

Crisp apples tumble, they roll and laugh,
As cider spills out from a friendly gaffe.
While witches rehearse their comedic spells,
On broomsticks they ride, ringing merry bells.

In alliteration, laughter ignites,
As autumn's humor sparkles and excites.
So join this delight, come take a chance,
In the land of mishaps, let's sing and dance!

Odes to the Overcast

The clouds above look quite bemused,
They wear their grays like silly hats.
A stormy tune they have produced,
While raindrops dance like acrobats.

Umbrellas flutter, quite absurd,
Like fish that flop, they twist and turn.
Each puddle's splash is quite the word,
As laugh out loud, the raindrops churn.

The sun peeks through with cheeky glee,
A game of hide-and-seek we play.
But don't you fret, don't you agree,
The gloomy sky can still be gay?

So, let us sing this cloudy tune,
Where every gray has something bright.
For laughter's found beneath the moon,
Even when skies forget the light.

Fragments of Frequencies

A radio crackles with delight,
Playing tunes from yesterday's spree.
Static hums a jolly fight,
While dance moves laugh with glee.

Each channel jumbles in a spin,
Do tunes from space just want to tease?
A cat meows, joins in the din,
While frogs croak their please and tease.

The beat drops down, and up it flies,
With every tick, it wiggles free.
Silly sounds, a twisty prize,
Musical mischief, no degree!

Let's tune in to this merry mess,
With giggles echoing like a tune.
For laughter's found in every stress,
In frequencies that end too soon.

Resonance of Radiance

The sunbeams play, a golden game,
Chasing shadows, shining bright.
Each sunny giggle has a name,
Tickling the flowers with delight.

With sunny hats that giggle loud,
Dandelions break into a cheer.
They sway, they bow, a funny crowd,
As butterflies flutter near.

The daisies dance a polka step,
Wiggling with a joyful twist.
While worms form lines, on earth they prep,
To join this sunny, vibrant list.

So come and bask in this warm glow,
Where laughter echoes in each ray.
Fun multiplied, with splendid flow,
In sunlight's arms, let joy hold sway.

Winding Words

Words swirl around like leaves in fall,
Twisting, turning, such a show!
Some tumble down, while others crawl,
A funny dance, oh, watch them go!

A word, it flips, and trips, and skips,
Spreading laughter through the air.
With silly puns and cheeky quips,
Each slip and slide, a frolic rare.

Their jumbled joy brings smiles anew,
A treasure hunt with every line.
They bounce around, an echo few,
Crafting chuckles with each sign.

So let us gather all these slots,
Where winding words create the fun.
For every twist that laughter plots,
Unleashes joy like morning sun!

Lines Lost in the Lush Overgrowth

In the garden where words play,
A lost line took a holiday.
It danced with daisies, spun with glee,
Until it met a bumblebee.

The bee buzzed loud, oh what a sound,
Each syllable twirled round and round.
The line exclaimed, 'Is this my fate?'
The bee just laughed, 'You're pretty late!'

A squirrel joined, so cheeky, spry,
He grabbed the line, said, 'Oh my!'
With acorns tossed, they made a spree,
An ode to mischief, wild and free.

But when the sun began to set,
The lost line wondered without fret,
For every turn, each bumpy nook,
Was better than a dusty book.

Symphony of Whispers beneath the Sun.

Underneath that glowing star,
Whispers danced, both near and far.
They tickled leaves, made shadows play,
Sprouting giggles, brightening the day.

A shout from grass — 'I've got a joke!'
The tree responded, 'Don't be a bloke!'
The breeze just chuckled, swirling light,
While flowers winked in sheer delight.

Then came a beetle with a grin,
He hummed a tune and joined right in.
Each verse a petal, light and spry,
Creating music with a sigh.

As laughter lifted, sunbeams glowed,
The whispers twirled in joy bestowed.
In that symphony, so whimsically spun,
We found our hearts full of pun.

Whispers of Words

In the forest, words take flight,
Frogs croak verses through the night.
With every hop, they rhyme and jump,
While crickets add a special thump.

Missed a line? Don't fret, my friend,
The wind will carry it to the end.
A chatterbox bird adds some flair,
With feathers flipping through the air.

A squirrel thinks, 'What's all this fuss?'
He waves his tail, creates a bus!
All aboard for silly rhymes,
We're traveling past the land of climes.

In the murmur, joy ignites,
The whispers twirl, and take their flights.
Through giggles, laughter, a brand-new day,
The words will always come to play.

Melody in the Leaves

In the breeze, a tune takes shape,
Leaves converge and begin to scrape.
Each rustling note, a comedy,
Bringing laughter, wild and free.

A leaf fell down, said, 'I'm a star!'
Rolling to earth — 'Hey, look at me far!'
With acorns clapping, tunes do sway,
In this leafy cabaret play.

But wait! A bird joined in for fun,
Singing high, under the sun.
The groundhog chuckled, danced with glee,
'You're not so shy, come swing with me!'

As day wore on, the trees all swayed,
In harmony, their laughter played.
Together they spun, this merry band,
Creating melodies, so unplanned.

Realm of Refrains

In a land where giggles bloom,
The sun wears a silly hat.
Dancing clouds, oh what a room,
With birds that chat and chat!

Silly socks are lost in time,
While llamas strut with flair.
Each rhyme a tasty slice of lime,
In joy, we find our share!

Bouncing balls of laughter roll,
Tickling toes of every beast.
Chasing shadows takes its toll,
But we're not quite finished, at least!

So let's frolic, skip, and rhyme,
In the realm of silly dreams.
Where every giggle's worth a dime,
And laughter's more than it seems!

Small Hours of Similes

Tickling the stars like feathers,
The moon winks behind a tree.
Nighttime chats wear cozy sweaters,
As squirrels sip their herbal tea.

Imagery leaps with silly grace,
Like frogs with shoes on every jump.
Each figure dances in its place,
While owls giggle with a thump!

Curly mustaches on sleepy cats,
Daydreams wearing polka dots.
Insomniac rats in top hats,
Share jokes that twist like knots.

So come join the quirky crew,
In small hours thick with fun.
Where words bounce and tumble too,
Until the rising sun!

Wandering Verses

Adventures lead through wobbly lanes,
Where puns explode like bubbles.
Juggling rhymes on bouncing trains,
Always ending in giggles and troubles.

Sneaky squirrels with hats on tight,
Plot mischief with a cheeky grin.
Each verse a dance, a silly flight,
In a world where nonsense begins!

Wandering words on a trampoline,
Flipping meanings upside down.
Sliding laughter, swift and keen,
In a jester's colorful gown.

So hop aboard, let's take a trip,
Through lines that tickle and tease.
With every rhyme, we start to skip,
In a landscape made to please!

Empyrean Echoes

High above where jesters sing,
The clouds wear shoes of rainbow hues.
Giggles bounce and laughter swings,
As butterflies spread silly news.

Echoes twirl on fluffy floors,
Like cupcakes flying 'round the sun.
Each rhyme a door to open shores,
Where puns and sweets are all in fun!

Napping stars with sleepy eyes,
Trade tickles for a wink or two.
While comets wear a big surprise,
In dances meant for giggling crews.

So sway with joy among the light,
In empyrean skies so bright.
Where every echo brings delight,
And laughter reigns throughout the night!

Whispers Among the Verses

In a land where words play, a jolly tune,
Jokes tiptoe lightly, like dancers at noon.
Puns giggle and chuckle, quite ready to tease,
They're sneaky like squirrels, swaying on trees.

A rhyme tries to prance, but trips on its feet,
It slips on a punchline; oh, isn't that sweet?
Verbs wear a smile, in their colorful garb,
While nouns roll their eyes, saying, "That's just a barb!"

Metaphors mingle at the half-moon's light,
Sharing their secrets, oh what a sight!
The alliteration laughs; it's a tongue-twisting spree,
As vowels and consonants dance with great glee.

So let us rejoice in this silly parade,
Where language is laughter, and puns never fade.
Join in the frolic, be silly, have fun,
For in the world of words, we're all number one!

Echoes of the Unspoken

In the silence, words lurk, like cats in the night,
Witty little whispers, ready to take flight.
Giggles of grammar, tip-tap on the floor,
While commas throw parties behind every door.

A pun walks a tightrope, with style and flair,
While similes snicker, without a single care.
Adjectives waltz in their dazzling costumes,
As they paint all the nouns with vibrant costumes.

Oh, the irony juggles as sarcasm spins,
While ellipses snicker at all of our sins.
An oxymoron skates with a wink and a grin,
Making sense of the nonsense, let the laughter begin!

So let's toast to the cheeky, the clever, the bright,
In this whimsical realm, where puns rule the night.
With echoes of laughter that bounce through the air,
Words dance in the twilight, no reason to care!

Serenade of Silenced Lines

In a garden of verses where giggles take root,
A cactus named Rhyme wears a glittery suit.
He pokes at the verses with humor so spry,
While puns swoop like birds, oh they flutter and fly!

Alliteration assembles, tapping its toes,
While metaphors marvel at how the wind blows.
One word shimmies forward, slips right on a rhyme,
And every little chuckle feels just so sublime.

A daffy apostrophe, bouncing on two,
Adds flair to the lines, oh what can it do?
It twirls and it sways with a cheerful decree,
As whispers turn into a raucous jubilee!

So gather your giggles, have fun, don't be shy,
In this serenade of laughter, let your worries fly.
For every bowed line has a story to share,
With a wink and a nod, we spread giggles everywhere!

Dance of the Words in Flight

Words pirouette lightly, in a salsa of fun,
They toss their twists gently, under the sun.
A verb on a trampoline, jumps with a grin,
While nouns in their spats, shout, "Let the dance begin!"

Each couplet glimmers in a spotlight bold,
As phrases parade, with stories untold.
The haikus hop forward, with steps ever neat,
While hashtags high-five, to a digital beat.

The stanzas all shimmy, they shake and they groove,
As rhythms resonate, and words find their move.
Conjunctions explode in a burst of delight,
While laughter is painted on canvases bright.

So join in the jive, let your spirit take flight,
In the dance of the words, we'll party all night.
Where humor ignites, like fireworks in bloom,
In this whimsical waltz, let your joy find a room!

Tidal Verses

Waves of words splash on the shore,
A seagull squawks, always wanting more.
With silly lines that dance and jig,
Watch them twirl like a plump fat pig.

Ocean's laughter bounces around,
Tidal tales make the sea feel sound.
Nautical nonsense, a sailor's spree,
Riding the waves of a rhyme-filled sea.

Droplets giggle, tickling toes,
Sandcastles crumble as the wind blows.
Splish and splash in whimsical glee,
Each wave a rhyme, wild and free!

Moonlight glimmers, a playful tease,
As ocean rhymes sway like the breeze.
A quirky tune sung to the night,
Oh, what a laugh with each moonlit bite!

Vibrations of Vistas

Hilly highs with silly sights,
Each curve a giggle, wild delights.
Bouncing bunnies hop with flair,
Chasing rainbows in the air.

Trees are winking with leafy grins,
Every rustle hints at twin tin twins.
Birds compose their chirpy choirs,
Melodies spark, igniting fires.

Clouds wearing hats of puffy white,
Dancing shadows in the golden light.
Nature giggles with every sway,
Painting humor in a funny way.

Mountains chuckle, valleys hum,
In this landscape, laughter's from the drum.
Silly sights with vibrant views,
Reality tickles in colorful hues!

Lyrical Landscapes

On the canvas of a sunny day,
Painted with words in a playful way.
A sunset giggles, blushes away,
As colors mix, they start to sway.

Fields of laughter, daisies spin,
Whirling round like they're topped with gin.
Every blade a clever tease,
Waving 'hello' with cheeky ease.

Puddles chuckle, reflections gleam,
Funny faces dance in a dream.
A hopscotch joy among the blooms,
Where laughter echoes from sunny rooms.

Clouds trade jokes in a fluffy flare,
As the breeze tickles through the air.
Lyrical things that make us grin,
Nature's stage where giggles begin!

Dreamweavers in the Dark

In the night, where shadows play,
Whimsical whispers lead the way.
Moonbeams dance with silly grace,
A laughter-filled and twinkly space.

Stars wear hats and winks, oh my!
Dreamweavers giggle and flutter by.
In this realm of nighttime cheer,
Every flicker gives a goofy leer.

Nightjars sing with boisterous tones,
Their melodies tickle like happy bones.
Cuddled under a velvet sky,
Where even the owls cant help but sigh.

Mystical dreams begin to swirl,
With every giggle, fantasies unfurl.
Laughter echoes through realms of dark,
With each whimsy, a joyful spark!

Tides of Ink and Imagination

Oh, the ink spills like tea on a floor,
Words float around like a fish on a shore.
Imagination winks in bright colored hues,
As vowels dance barefoot in mismatched shoes.

Scribbles tumble down like cats on a spree,
Puns pirouette, swirling all wild and free.
Each phrase a balloon that takes flight with a cheer,
While commas play tag, giggling near.

A writer's delight, with ideas that gleam,
Creating a world that's a whimsical dream.
A paper boat sails down a river of thought,
Bumping into the verses that laughter has sought.

Full of mischief and scribbles galore,
The pages erupt with giggles galore.
With waves of pure joy, they crash and collide,
As imagination and ink take a fun-filled ride.

Lullabies from Leafy Canopies

Up in the trees where the squirrels hold court,
The leaves sing softly, a nutty retort.
Each rustle a giggle, each branch a piano,
As chipmunks compose an acorn-sized canto.

The sunlight peeks in with a tickle and tease,
While the branches nod dance and sway in the breeze.
Mushrooms giggle quietly, dressed in their best,
Inviting all critters to join in the fest.

Nature's own choir with frogs in the mix,
Croaking out rhythms and silly ol' tricks.
With insects as dancers tapping their feet,
They twist and they twirl in a leafy retreat.

So come take a nap where the laughter is light,
Under the canopy, where dreams take their flight.
With lullabies whispered by critters and trees,
Cuddled by nature's soft melodies, please!

Chimes of Connection in the Air

In the garden of laughter where whispers collide,
Chimes of connection soar far and wide.
With each gentle jingle, a joke takes to wing,
As flowers all chuckle, their petals a-swinging.

The bees buzz in tune, a winged symphony,
While butterflies flutter, sipping on glee.
In the chorus of colors, they all play a part,
Connecting their giggles straight to the heart.

A playful breeze tickles the flowers so bright,
Sending seeds of joy on a whimsical flight.
While vines intertwine in a comical dance,
Nature's grand party invites us to prance.

So come feel the magic; let laughter prevail,
In this garden of wonders, where jokes never fail.
With chimes of connection ringing so clear,
A melody of fun that's music to hear!

Fables in the Fragrant Gale

Under the breeze where the stories are spun,
Fables take flight, giggling just for fun.
With scents of the flowers tickling the nose,
Each tale blooms like magic where laughter grows.

A bear shares a yarn, with a twinkle in eye,
About a dancing porcupine passing by.
The flowers all chuckle, their petals a burst,
While bees seek the nectar, laughing their thirst.

Each story a tickle, each fable a jest,
Where the skies are all painted in humor's best.
The shadows join in, play peek-a-boo games,
As giggles and grins spread like fluffy flames.

So sway with the stories, let laughter enthrall,
In the fragrant gale, hear the giggles call.
With fables so funny, cascading like rain,
Life's quirks and delights dance across the plain.

Ethereal Envelopes

In a world where letters drift,
Dancing through the air, they shift.
Paper planes with jokes inside,
Tickle your ribs, like laughter wide.

An envelope with wings takes flight,
Chasing giggles day and night.
Stamps that giggle, seals that grin,
Postcards whisper, 'Let the fun begin!'

Bubbles burst with silly claims,
Each message writ in jumbled names.
Ink that squirts like silly goo,
Sending smiles from me to you.

Floating notes of quirky cheer,
Carried off to far and near.
Ethereal jokes in each address,
Life's a joke, it's just a mess.

Alphabet Soup Serenade

In a bowl of letters, we're afloat,
Swirling sounds like a little boat.
Spelling giggles with every slurp,
Spoonful of fun, watch the noodles burp!

A dash of 'A' and a pinch of 'B',
Creating chaos, oh can't you see?
Each sip a song, a soup-tastic dance,
Swallowed whole in a noodle trance!

Spoon-stirred sonnets, bubbling bright,
Kitchen concerts, what a sight!
Croutons giggling, broth so warm,
Each bite a laugh, a noodle swarm!

Alphabet soup, a silly spree,
Making meals a comedy.
Serving laughs with every taste,
Silly letters, never waste.

Serpentining Sonnets

Wiggle and writhe, the lines entwine,
Slithering words like a serpentine.
Tongue-tied tigers, a twisted rhyme,
Chasing laughter through the slime.

Sonnets dance in a wiggly spree,
Words like snakes, so wild and free.
Each verse curls and forms a tail,
A wriggly giggle in a poetic trail.

Twisting tales of giggling snakes,
Jokes that leave you in bellyaches.
Poetry with a wobbly bend,
Silly sonnets that never end.

Serpentining lines in a playful crawl,
Making you chuckle, the best of all.
A slippery slip of fun in each jest,
Sonnets that wiggle, a playful quest.

Waltz of Words

In a grand hall of jumbled speech,
Words twirl around, just out of reach.
Linguistic dancers in mismatched shoes,
Shuffling rhymes, singing the blues.

Waltzing whispers under the bright light,
Each line a jiggle, pure delight.
Giggles twirling, laughter in flight,
A comedy ball in the clear moonlight.

Pages flutter like skirts in a rush,
Words collide with a goofy hush.
Scribbled stories that spin and swirl,
Dancing letters in a playful whirl.

A waltz of nonsense, a jovial spree,
Each stanza a giggle, wild and free.
Step to the rhythm of crazed rhyme,
Join the dance, it's wordy time!

Petals in Poetry

In the garden of words, where giggles bloom,
Each line curls up, like a kitten in gloom.
Verses dance gaily, wearing shoes untied,
Chasing butterflies, with laughter as their guide.

A daffodil whispers a joke to a rose,
While tulips plot mischief, nobody knows.
Bees hum a tune, with a buzz and a spin,
In this rhyming affair, let the fun begin!

The daisies all tumble, in a grand parade,
While the sun gives a wink, as if it had played.
Petals in pockets, confetti on cake,
In this playful garden, all rules can break.

Laughter is pollen, drifting through the air,
Words flutter about, without a single care.
Each stanza a petal, on a warm summer day,
In the fun of the lines, we will frolic and play.

Chimes of Change

The clock strikes a laugh, with a tick-tock glee,
As pendulums swing, to an unknown decree.
Time jests and jives, with a wink in its eye,
Turning minutes to mush, where giggles can fly.

An hourglass dances, with sand made of cheer,
Shaking off worries, as time gets sincere.
Wind chimes are laughing, as they clang and ring,
Announcing the joy that each moment can bring.

Calendars chuckle, as weeks turn to fun,
Each day is a joke, under the bright sun.
For every tick forward, a giggle we gain,
In the chimes of this life, we keep dancing in vain.

So let's turn the page, on this chapter of now,
With laughter as ink, we'll paint wonders somehow.
Change is just humor, dressed up in disguise,
As we jive in the rhythm, that time sweetly supplies.

Chorus of the Currents

The river sings softly, with splashes of fun,
As fish do a two-step, beneath the warm sun.
Water tickles rocks, in a giggling spree,
Each ripple a rhyme, as it sways joyfully.

Leaves on the trees join the melody sweet,
With swirls of the breeze, happy notes they repeat.
Crickets play percussion, with their chirps so loud,
In this lively chorus, we dance with the crowd.

A splash from a frog, with a leap and a croak,
Sends laughter ricocheting, like a favorite joke.
Nature's own symphony, a delightful fright,
In the currents of joy, everything feels right.

The sky joins the laughter, in clouds fluffy white,
As stars wink at us, when it turns into night.
In this chorus of cheer, let the moments unfold,
With giggles and splashes, let the tales be retold.

Palette of the Past

In an attic of memories, colors collide,
Each hue tells a story, with laughter as guide.
Crayons enlisted, with winks in their tips,
Painting old moments, with giggles and slips.

A canvas of chaos, with sketches a mess,
Each stroke is a chuckle, with a hint of finesse.
Old photos do shuffle, in a frame they once knew,
As whiskers on kittens play tag with a shoe.

The brush dips in laughter, as it happily sways,
Recreating the past, in whimsical ways.
Memories swirl, in a polka-dot dance,
Mixing joy with the colors, giving life a chance.

So let's splash these hues, onto life's grand wall,
With silly mishaps, that shall never fall.
Each shade is a chuckle, woven into time,
In this palette of joy, we'll keep making rhyme.

Tapestry of Time

In the garden, time slipped by,
A snail in a hurry, oh my oh my!
The daisies giggle, the sun gives a wink,
Dancing shadows make us rethink.

With every tick, the clock's a clown,
Wearing its hands like a floppy gown.
Jumping from hour to hour with glee,
Who knew time loved to play tag, you see?

Old tales of yore pop up with flair,
Even history's memes give a fair share.
Butterflies flutter, they swing and sway,
In this wild tapestry, they giggle away.

So come take a seat, grab some delight,
In the tapestry of time that's a pure sight.
With laughter and love we knit day by day,
Making memories in the funniest way.

Harmonies of Hope

A chicken sings, it's quite a tune,
Clucking along beneath the moon.
A melody rises, the barn's a stage,
Where hopes take flight, uncaged and brave.

Pigs in tuxedos groove to the beat,
While cows play the drums with their big, meaty feet.
In this silly barnyard, we tap our toes,
As dreams bounce around like a flock of crows.

The sun peeks in with a wink and a grin,
Lighting up laughter, let the fun begin!
Dance with the daisies, skip with the breeze,
In this harmony, it's all a tease.

So join the chorus of joy and cheer,
Where every little laugh is music to hear.
In this funny symphony, let's find our hope,
With rhythms so quirky, we'll learn to cope.

Rhapsody in the Rain

Raindrops tap-dance on my old tin roof,
Making a rhythm that's quite the goof.
Puddles reflect a circus of dreams,
Where umbrellas compete in silly schemes.

With each little splash, the world does cheer,
Who knew raindrops could bring such cheer?
Jump in the puddles, lose your shoes,
In this symphony, we've nothing to lose.

Clouds wear their coats, all mismatched and funny,
Dripping with laughter, oh so sunny!
A duck quacks a tune, a joyful refrain,
In the rhapsody of our playful rain.

So let's twirl and swirl, in wet delight,
Chasing rainbows until it's night.
In every droplet, let's find our chance,
To dance in the rain and romp and prance.

Cadence of the Cosmos

Stars wear hats made of twinkling light,
Doing a jig in the deep, dark night.
The moon is an ace at playing charades,
As planets do pirouettes in their parades.

Neptune's painted nails shine bright like gems,
While comets whistle delightful hymns.
Each galaxy spins in a swirling spree,
Painting the cosmos so wittily.

Eclipses wave like they're playing peek-a-boo,
Jupiter jokes with his thunderous crew.
The Milky Way giggles, a twist of fate,
In this cosmic dance, we celebrate.

So squeeze your friends and look to the skies,
With laughter and wonder, let's be wise.
In the cadence of the cosmos, stories unfold,
Filled with laughter, adventure untold.

Chasing Chords

The cat danced a jig, oh what a foul sound,
While the dog tried to bark, fell right to the ground.
Dancing shoes mismatched, a party gone wrong,
They twisted and twirled to a wobbly song.

The mouse brought some cheese, thought it a delight,
But the cat's silly prance sent him off in a fright.
With a leap and a squeak, he vanished for good,
While the dog chased his tail in the neighborhood.

A jolly old parrot joined in the spree,
Squawking out rhymes that made no sense, whee!
With a flap and a flap, a whirlwind of fluff,
This musical chaos was simply enough.

So here's to the chords that we chase every day,
In the dance of our lives, let the laughter play.
With mismatched shoes and a tune out of tune,
We'll be silly forever, like a bright afternoon.

Patterns of Poetry

In the garden of words, a bee took a seat,
Buzzing a rhyme, that was quite the feat.
A ladybug danced as it whispered a pun,
While a lazy old snail still was weighing the fun.

The sun wore a hat, it was comically bright,
Telling the clouds, 'You won't spoil my plight!'
The flowers were laughing, heads bobbing with glee,
As a worm made a face, 'Why not me in the spree?'

Each petal composed its own little line,
Crafting sweet verses as if they were fine.
With laughter like poetry, life took a cue,
Chasing silliness under skies so blue.

So let's join the dance, let our patterns unfold,
In the book of the world, let the stories be told.
With petals and laughter, in gardens we stay,
Creating a ruckus in our own silly way.

Reflections in Rhyme

A mirror once chuckled, oh what a surprise,
It cracked at the sight of two googly eyes.
The face on the left, with a wink and a grin,
Said, 'Did you see that? Let the fun now begin!'

A frog joined the party, leaping quite high,
Croaking out limericks beneath the blue sky.
The fish in the pond sang gurgling notes,
While a cat played the keys with its tiny little toes.

In the midst of the laughter, a sight to behold,
The reflections grew giddy, their antics so bold.
Each twist and each turn brought a smirk and a cheer,
In a world where the silly was perfectly clear.

So let's raise our voices with echoes so sweet,
In the dance of reflection, let's tap our own beat.
With mirrors and laughter, let joy intertwine,
Creating a symphony, pure fun within rhyme.

Rhythms of Remembrance

The clock chimed a tune, totally absurd,
Ticking in salsa, oh what a word!
With winks and with nudges, the moments took flight,
As a chicken and fox danced far into night.

Old boots found a partner, both squeaked in delight,
Twirling in rhythm, oh what a sight!
They bookended friendship, mismatched yet true,
Creating a memory, shared by the crew.

With each little giggle, the moments aligned,
In the archives of laughter, where joy is defined.
A sandwich recounted its time on the plate,
As the pickles chimed in, 'Just you wait, just you wait!'

These rhythms of memory, they wobble and sway,
In a dance that reminds us of life's funny play.
So gather your stories, let laughter draw near,
In the scrapbook of time, may we always hold dear.

Verses of the Wind

The leaves start to giggle, they tickle my toes,
As breezes blow softly, and nobody knows.
A squirrel tells secrets to clouds up above,
While dandelions dance in the sun, full of love.

The whispers of grasses, so green and so bright,
Spin stories of moonbeams that twinkle at night.
A butterfly chuckles, it's silly to glide,
As I join the parade, with laughter as my guide.

The trees sway in rhythm, they wiggle and bend,
A chorus of nature, oh what a blend!
The wind winks at flowers, their petals applaud,
In this giggling garden, we're all a bit odd.

When raindrops fall gently, they dance on my hat,
A symphony swells, every drop, a chitchat.
With chuckles and snickers, I tread on the ground,
In this playful ballet, where giggles abound.

Serenade of Silhouettes

In twilight's embrace, the shadows take shape,
With dances of silliness, oh what a tape!
The trees start to prance, with topsy-turvy moves,
While moonbeams giggle, in silly grooves.

A cat on a fence, wearing boots two sizes too small,
Swings tail like a lasso, ready to fall.
The stars join in laughter, a twinkling brigade,
As night holds a concert, of whimsy displayed.

The owls hoot a tune, all wise and bemused,
As crickets contribute, like poets, confused.
The silhouettes sway, in a comical trance,
A parade of the quirky, in night's merry dance.

With a flick of their tails, and an upside-down grin,
The shadows keep prancing, let the shenanigans begin!
As dawn tiptoes in, with a yawn and a stretch,
The serenade pauses, till next time we sketch.

Echoes of Enchantment

In the depths of the forest, where giggles reside,
The echoes bounce playfully, a chorus of pride.
With mushrooms like stools, and fairies on chairs,
They whisper and chuckle, with upturned affairs.

A rabbit with glasses keeps counting the stars,
While bees wear tuxedos, and dance with guitars.
The whispers of wonders, enchant each curvy lane,
With sprinkles of laughter that fall like sweet rain.

The toadstools tap dance, on bubbles of air,
In the kingdom of mirth, with giggles to spare.
Each echo reflects, a twist in the tale,
As creatures commingle, a whimsical trail.

So shout to the moon, with a voice loud and clear,
For enchantment is waiting, there's nothing to fear!
With a tickle from twilight, let the laughter ignite,
In our echoes of wonder, we frolic till night.

Dance of the Dactyls

In a rhythm of chuckles, the dactyls take flight,
With patterns of giggles, making chaos feel right.
Each step with a bounce, oh how they delight,
Tickling the funny bone, with joy that feels bright.

They shimmy like jelly, so wiggly and free,
Tick-tocks of laughter, as wild as can be.
The sun gives a wink, as shadows all play,
While the dactyls keep dancing, come join the fray!

With a twirl and a whirl, they spin through the air,
Their song full of nonsense, a humorous flare.
The trees sway in chorus, the clouds join the tune,
As the dance of the dactyls makes magic at noon.

So jive with the funny, let your laughter be bold,
In this whimsical fiesta, where giggles unfold.
From dawn till the dusk, keep your spirit awake,
For the dance is contagious, let merriment quake!

www.ingramcontent.com/pod-product-compliance
Lightning Source LLC
Chambersburg PA
CBHW051645160426
43209CB00004B/797